APPLIED zen

Oakwood Publishing, a division of
Zaltho Foundation, Inc.
550 Mary Esther Cut Off NW, PMB 319
Fort Walton Beach, FL. 32548

Copyright © 2025 by Claude A. Thomas

Proceeds from the sale of this book will be donated to
the Zaltho Foundation.

All rights reserved. No part of this publication, including artwork,
may be reproduced in any form or by any means, electronic or physical,
without prior written permission from the Zaltho Foundation, Inc.

Cover and interior design by Hilary Harkness

Image page 32 by Olympia Davies on Unsplash

Library of Congress Control Number: 2024948829

ISBN paperback 978-1-7362934-7-8
ISBN ebook 978-1-7362934-8-5

APPLIED Zen

A Short Guide to an Active Meditation Practice

CLAUDE ANSHIN THOMAS

MARY ESTHER, FLORIDA

"On the great road of buddha ancestors there is always unsurpassable practice, continuous and sustained. It forms the circle of the Way and is never cut off.... The power of this continuous practice confirms you as well as others. It means your practice affects the entire earth and the entire sky in the ten directions.... By your continuous practice, the continuous practice of all buddhas is actualized and the great road of all buddhas opens up."

—Dogen, *Shobogenzo*

Contents

A Few Words to the Reader	ix
An Introduction to Practice	1
Sitting Meditation	7
Bowing	17
The Altar	21
Walking Meditation	27
Eating Meditation	33
Working Meditation	37
Deep Listening and Mindful Speech	41
Sleeping Meditation	47
Leave No Trace	51
Be On Time	55
Doorway Practice	59
Goodbye Meditation	63
Conclusion	67
About the Author	73
Also Available	76

A Few Words to the Reader

I have written this book for those seeking simple, concrete spiritual tools to support them in their daily lives, those who want to begin to do something immediately to change their lives and thereby the world we live in. These simple practices have grown as a result of my commitment to heal from the devastating effects of childhood violence and the consequences of being a combat soldier during the war in Vietnam. They have grown out of a deep and burning desire to live my life differently. These are the daily practices that have supported me as I engage with the Buddha's teachings in highly practical ways, in all of my affairs, letting this take me where it will.

I have not written *Applied Zen* to entertain or provide intellectual stimulation. I have written this book to offer some basic tools that can support us in awakening to and embodying our enlightened nature. Meditation practice is not about enjoyment. Go deeper than your ideas of enjoyment. Stay with it, stay with the process. Breathe into your abdomen, breathe out. Keep going and don't give up. Then you will begin to experience the benefit. Meditation brings you right into contact with your resistance. This is important. Resistance and doubt are an important and valuable part of the process. When you experience these so-called obstacles, just continue to sit and see what unfolds.

In Zen practice, we must develop an unwavering commitment to waking up while at the same time abandoning any ideas or preconceptions about what this awakening will look like or how it will impact us. On the path of practice, we must also be patient and sensitive with ourselves for the actions that we take in forgetfulness; we must be gentle with ourselves without becoming lazy or making excuses.

My commitment is to be of service. So, may I be of service to you through this text.

APPLIED zen

An Introduction to Practice

Meditation doesn't have just one form. It is not only something we do seated on a cushion or a chair—it is a way of life. We learn and practice specific forms of meditation in order to wake up to the reality that spiritual practice and daily life are not two separate things.

By living a life rooted in meditation, we have the opportunity to recognize our repeating patterns of suffering and begin to establish a more conscious relationship with these patterns so that they no longer control us. Through this process, through living a life rooted in a disciplined and committed meditation practice, we have the opportunity to fully experience the wonder of being alive.

Meditation is not medication. It will not rescue us from our pain, from our moods. It is not for escaping our discomfort or for fixing ourselves. Meditation is about facing ourselves—about developing the courage and commitment to be present with our thoughts, feelings, and perceptions on an ongoing basis, no matter what we're doing. When we live this way, when we bring meditation practice into all aspects of our lives, we gradually come to discover our innate wisdom and our essential unbrokenness.

Why practice meditation?
Because the path to liberation rests in discipline. Discipline is not a rigid way of living one's life. (Rigidness is a form of suffering.) Discipline is a commitment to engaging with specific practice forms on a daily basis, practices that support us in training the mind and living our lives with more awareness. When I speak of training the mind, I am not referring to the intellect. That is only one aspect of the mind. The mind in the spiritual sense is the totality of what we call experience. It is everything and everywhere.

Just for a moment, abandon your habitual way of thinking and try on a new way of perceiving the world. Just for this moment consider that here, in this precise moment and in this exact space, exists the entire universe. There is nothing else and nowhere else.

The different forms of meditation practice, along with rituals and teachings, support us in establishing a discipline that helps us to wake up to the realities of our lives, to the nature of suffering, to how we continue to perpetuate that suffering, and to how we can bring an end to that suffering.

In the Zen tradition in which I practice and teach, the different forms of meditation include: sitting meditation, walking meditation, working meditation, eating meditation, speaking-and-listening meditation, bowing, and silence. We practice these forms so that we can become aware of the essential fact that the way we care for anything in our world—the kitchen sink, our shoes, our toothbrush—is vitally important. We practice to become aware that this is no less or no more important than anything else that we do. We practice to learn how to pay attention to the smallest detail or particle and to the largest space, because in the smallest particle exists the largest space, and in the largest space exists the smallest particle.

I am not interested in how deeply you bow or how well you can speak the language of Dharma or how much Buddhist jewelry you wear. None of that makes a bit of difference if you don't make your bed each morning. It doesn't make any difference if you don't wash your clothes with care and attention. It doesn't make any difference if you are always angry. It doesn't make any difference if you are harming yourself and others each day by smoking cigarettes or if you hide within yourself in fear.

What matters is learning to practice sitting meditation in a way that supports us in living differently. If you want to wake up, if you want to learn the tools of meditation, I am very glad that you are reading this text.

Be aware

I cannot actually teach you meditation. Meditation can only be learned through experiencing it for yourself in an ongoing, committed way. I can provide you with instructions for the forms, as they were passed on to me by my teachers, as well as my experience with them. However, meditation is what happens when you sincerely and deeply engage in the forms. It happens within yourself and is your own personal experience.

I have had the opportunity to offer meditation instruction in a wide variety of settings to people from many different backgrounds. Wherever I go, I teach the Zen Buddhist practices that have helped me to transform my life, the same essential practices described in this book. I encourage you to engage whole heartedly with all of these practice forms so that we can all become the healing and peace we want to see in the world.

Sitting Meditation

Each morning and each evening practice sitting meditation for at least five minutes. Find a comfortable, quiet place and, if you like, create a small altar with a candle, incense, and some flowers. (Further instructions on creating and maintaining an altar are found on page 13.) You can sit in a chair, on the edge of your bed, or on the floor on a cushion or meditation bench.

If you sit on a chair, or something else that is elevated, place your feet flat on the floor in front of you, with your knees about hip width apart (your knees should not be held tightly together nor spread loosely apart). Do not lean against the back of the chair. Instead, sit on the front half of the seat so that your back is erect.

If you sit on the floor, you can sit in the full lotus, the half-lotus, or the Burmese Lotus position, using a cushion to lift up your bottom so that your knees can more easily touch the floor or mat. Or you can sit in seiza (the position that is frequently used among the monastic and lay practitioners in Japan), meaning kneeling and sitting on your heels. This position can be difficult for the beginner, so it may be helpful to place a cushion or meditation bench under your bottom.

Whether on a cushion or chair, sit with your back erect and shoulders back slightly (though not rigidly so), notice the natural curvature of your spine. Lower your chin slightly, elongating the back of the neck. Visualize your ears being aligned with your shoulders and your nose aligned with your navel. In sitting meditation, correct posture is important for many reasons, including the fact that it facilitates easy flow of the breath.

Find a comfortable position for your hands, such as resting them on your lap. Or you could take the more traditional approach of placing the back of your left hand into the palm of your right hand, with thumbs almost touching. If you choose this position, allow your hands to rest gently on your thighs.

You can sit with your eyes open or closed. If you leave them open, pick a spot on the floor in front of you, lower your gaze, and let your eyes rest there. From this posture, focus your attention on your breath, each in-breath and each out-breath. As you breathe, pay attention to the precise point where the breath enters the body and then the precise point where it exits the body. Be sure to breathe into your abdomen, notice it expanding when you breathe in and contracting when you breathe out.

In sitting meditation there is nothing to be accomplished, nothing to be gained. As thoughts and feelings arise and perceptions are formed, simply notice them. Don't attach yourself to them and don't reject them. If your attention wanders, just return the focus of your awareness to your breath. The goal is not to stop our thinking but to recognize when we have become lost in thought and to reestablish a conscious connection to the breath.

If you discover that you are having difficulty staying focused on your breath, use the technique of counting your breaths as a support. Take one in-breath and one out-breath, and silently count "one"; in, out, "two," and so forth, until you reach ten. Once you have reached ten then count backwards to one. Keep in mind that the point is not getting to ten but staying connected to your breath.

If you experience physical discomfort, sit with that for a few moments. Don't immediately surrender to the urge to move, to restless energy. If the discomfort persists, then slowly shift your sitting posture slightly until the discomfort is relieved. Your "sitting muscles" (these are mental and spiritual as well as physical) will get stronger after some practice.

Practice each day, no matter what

Sit each morning and each evening, without question, for at least five minutes. It doesn't have to be perfect, but it is important that you do it. If you stick with this practice in a disciplined and consistent way, I guarantee your life will begin to transform.

Each period of meditation is different for me. What remains constant is concentrating on my breath. Sometimes I still wonder about this. I think, "What is the value of just placing my awareness on the breath?" Thoughts like this come and go.

There is no correct or ideal experience when we practice meditation. There is only the presentness that can exist in an active meditation practice. When we crave after some idea of meditation, we cannot be present. When sitting in meditation there is only noticing, without rejecting and without attaching. There is only the knowing that there is nothing to be achieved, nothing to be gained. Just stay in contact with the breath and pay attention.

I have been practicing sitting meditation, in one form or another, for more than four decades, and it wasn't until about ten years or so that I became able to sit without physical discomfort. But during those initial decades I continued to just sit and work with my body, allowing it to inform me. I experimented with different sitting positions: sitting in *seiza* (knees forward), on benches, in half-lotus. I tried all sorts of things over the years, and suddenly it just worked. I have no idea what happened. Something changed, and I could just sit for hours without any real difficulty. But then a few years ago my knees needed surgery. Right after the surgery I could not do prostrations or sit on a cushion. I still don't have the flexibility that I had before the surgery, but I am now able to do prostrations, and I can sit on a cushion with some extra support for my knees.

If you experience pain during sitting meditation, it is important to listen to your body, letting go of fixed ideas of how things have to be or have to look. When I am thinking too much, I cannot hear what my body is telling me. It is about really wanting to sit, then listening and experimenting, finding out what works.

The whole process of waking up is rooted in truly wanting to live differently. It doesn't matter how strong the conditioning is or what the obstacles are. What matters is the desire. The wanting. Even with significant injuries, I have found a way, by listening to my body, because I want to live differently. I have no fixed idea about what living differently will mean or what it might look like, none at all. It's always a process of listening and adjusting.

ALTERNATIVE POSTURES FOR SITTING MEDITATION

Half Lotus

Full Lotus

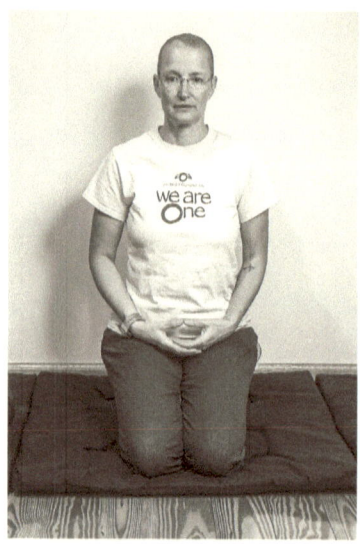

Seiza on bench

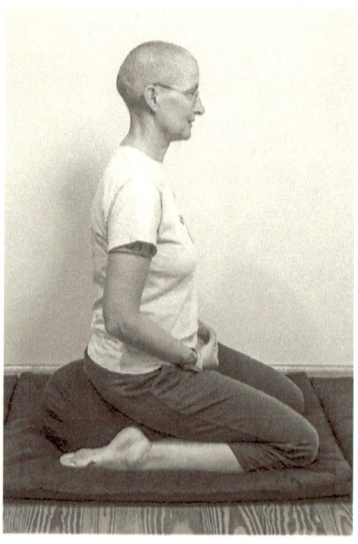

Seiza on cushion

ALTERNATIVE POSTURES FOR SITTING MEDITATION

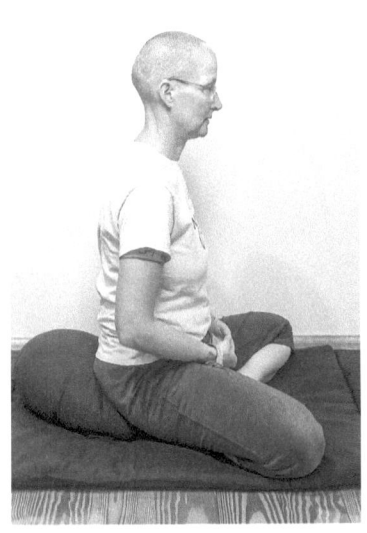

Side view, seated on a cushion

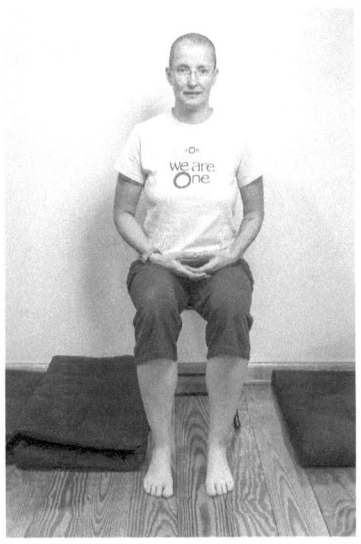

Seated in a chair

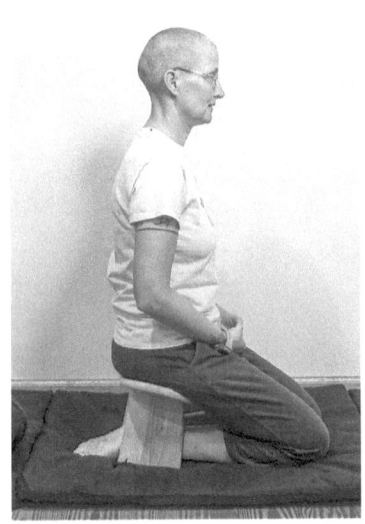

Side view, seated on
a meditation bench

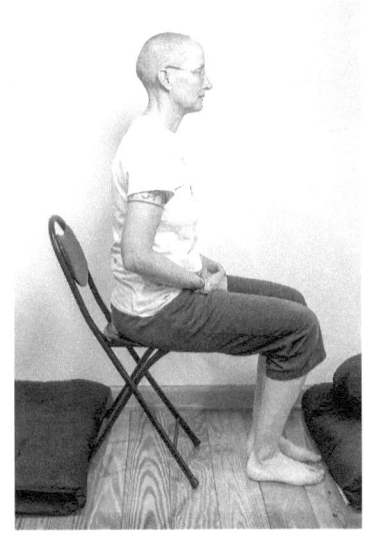

Side view, seated in a chair

Sitting Meditation 13

TRUE BOWING

"Dogen Zenji once said: 'As long as there is true bowing, the Buddha Way will not deteriorate.' In bowing, we totally pay respect to the all-pervading virtue of wisdom, which is the Buddha. In making the bow, we should move neither hastily nor sluggishly but simply maintain a reverent mind and humble attitude. When we bow too fast, the bow is then too casual a thing; perhaps we are even hurrying to get it over and done with. This is frequently the result of a lack of reverence. On the other hand, if our bow is too slow, then it becomes a rather pompous display; we may have gotten too attached to the feeling of bowing, or our own (real or imagined) gracefulness of movement. This is to have lost the humble attitude which a true bow requires."

—*Taizan Maezumi Roshi, On Zen Practice*

Bowing

In the first Zen monastery where I lived and studied, I was instructed on how and when to bow. I was told to press my palms together with my palms and fingertips touching. I was to then rest my thumbs on the knuckles of my index fingers, and the tips of my longest fingers were to be parallel with the tip of my nose. In Japanese, the name of this position is gassho.

The form was not to be too rigid or too relaxed. I was to place my hands at a comfortable distance from my body, not extended too far away nor too close. When bowing I was told to bow at the waist, keeping my eyes engaged with the person or object to which I was bowing. No other part of my body was to move.

Upon entering the meditation hall, I was instructed to step through the doorway with my right foot first and then bow in this manner to the space itself. I was then to go to my sitting place and bow toward my cushion and then to turn (in such a way that I would never show my back to the altar) and bow to the person sitting across from me. I was also instructed to bow when the teacher or person leading the practice period entered the meditation hall, which was announced with the sound of a bell.

At the time I felt great resistance to all of this. I suffered immensely from my preconceived notions of what bowing represented. I thought bowing was an act of subjugation, a sign of being below another person. So, I defiantly resisted following instructions. I stubbornly refused to bow to anyone or anything.

However, one day, still consumed by my suffering, I entered the meditation hall and, looking around to make sure that I was not being observed, I half-heartedly bowed. I noticed that I did not feel diminished. I continued this half-hearted experiment in bowing until on one day, just before I entered the meditation hall, I heard a clear, calm inner voice encouraging me to let go of my resistance and just bow. I thought, *What's the harm?* I can always stop bowing. I placed my hands in gassho, as instructed, and I stepped into the meditation hall with my right foot first. At the moment that my left foot joined my right foot I bowed. When I stood upright again, I was flooded with a rush of feelings. I burst into tears. I experienced a lightness of being that I did not know existed, a freedom from suffering that arose from bowing just to bow.

Since then I have come to appreciate the power of bowing practice in the process of waking up. It invites me to experience a powerful, sensitive, and engaged connection with whomever or whatever I am bowing to. I no longer see it as a gesture of submission—just the opposite. Today I see it as a way to honor the potential for awakening that exists in each and every one of us.

The Altar

To create a home altar, place a statue or image of the Buddha in the center of a table or shelf so that it is elevated slightly above the other elements of the altar. To the left of the Buddha, place a flower or plant. Directly in front of and below the Buddha, place a small bowl of water and directly in front of that place an incense holder (this could be a small bowl of ash, sand, uncooked rice, or earth). To the right of the Buddha, place a candle.

Before I approach the altar in the meditation hall, I do a standing bow to it. In doing this, I am bowing to all that the altar represents. Also acknowledging that the altar is not other than our body. Each item placed there represents one of the five elements, the building blocks of our bodies: the incense represents air, the air that we breath that is essential to life; the candle represents fire, or the essential energy that allows our body to function; the bowl of water (naturally) represents water, our body is something like 70% water; the flower represents earth, which contains the essential elements and minerals that are a building block of our body; and the Buddha represents space or consciousness. These five elements are what make life in this existence possible. Bowing at the altar, I am acknowledging the totality of existence and that my own body is made up of these elements, that I am not separate from them.

In our meditation hall at the Magnolia Zen Center, on either side of the Buddha are small statues representing various bodhisattvas. To the left of the Buddha is Avalokiteshavara (also known as Kanzeon or Guanyin), the bodhisattva of compassion and deep listening. To the right of the Buddha is Kshitigarbha (also known as Jizo or Earth Store bodhisattva), the rescuer of beings trapped in hell realms. Also supporting the transmigration from a hell realm.

At the beginning and end of practice periods or services, I do a full bow (a prostration) in front of the altar. I lower myself to the ground, placing my forehead on the floor and the backs of my hands on the ground near my ears, palms up. From there I slide my hands in front of me and then raise them off the floor slightly, ensuring that my palms remain flat and parallel to the ground at all times. As I do this, I am visualizing that I am gently sliding my hands underneath the seated Buddha. When I raise my hands off the floor I am lifting the Buddha up, elevating the Buddha above me, thereby honoring the awareness/consciousness that the Buddha represents. This awareness/consciousness is also available to me and to each and every one of us. I then carefully lower my hands to the floor, visualizing that I am placing the Buddha back down on the earth. I then slide my hands backward to a point just in front of my head removing them from under the Buddha.

To lift the Buddha above me is a reminder of my commitment to awaken. It is a reminder of my willingness and

intention to enter into an enlightened state and to embody that consciousness and awareness, a state empty of preconceptions. Prostrations are not an idle practice but one that requires and promotes the development of concentration. Many people who engage in this practice at first don't do it with much precision. They simply place the back of their hands on the floor and then bend their arms up at the elbow so that their palms end up near their shoulders. Doing this, they are, in essence, throwing the Buddha over their shoulders. It's important to visualize what one is doing during a full prostration and to cultivate an awareness of one's body in space.

Bringing consciousness into the action of bowing and the rituals of practice is to bring consciousness into all the actions of our daily lives. In reality, the actions of daily life are not other than ritual. All of the Zen Buddhist rituals we learn and practice have a purpose behind them. However, in the beginning it's important to simply engage in the rituals just to engage in them. As we become more accomplished, more familiar, our understanding will grow and any resistance to these practices will begin to melt away. At this point the true questions will appear, and when we receive responses to our questions these responses will be more clearly understood.

I do the opening rituals and practice of prostrations a bit differently than it was done in the Soto Zen center where I was trained. I put on my kesa (my formal monk's robe) in front of the altar and the people I am practicing with. (During my training, I would have entered the zendo already wearing my kesa.) I do this gesture publically to offer this ritual to the entire space and community. I place my folded robe on my head and sit in seiza, silently reciting the Verse of the Robe three times: "Vast is the robe of liberation, a formless field of benefaction, I wear the Tathagata teaching, saving all sentient beings." Then I carefully unfold and put on the kesa. Each day, whether I'm in the meditation hall or not, before I put on my robe or my rakusu (the smaller, daily robe) I place the robe on my head, and I recite the Verse of the Robe. This expresses and renews the commitment that I accept whenever I wear the robe.

Why so much attention to the robe? The robe represents the "Tathatgata teaching" or the dharma, so I am at once demonstrating my humility before it and the reality of my interconnectedness with it. What is the dharma? It is the truth, the universal truth that lies beyond the intellect, the truth that connects all things. The dharma is the suchness or essence of all that is.

After putting on the robe, I approach the left side of the altar with my hands in gassho. When I arrive at the altar, I step in front of each icon, do a standing bow, and silently recite, "I bow to you…" inserting multiple names by which each icon is known. (For example, when I'm in front of the bodhisattva Avalokiteshvara, I recite, "I bow to you, Avalokiteshvara Bodhisattva. I bow to you Guanyin Bodhisattva. I bow to you Kanzeon Bodhisattva.") When I'm directly in front of the Buddha, I also offer (or simulate offering) a small pinch of granulated incense onto a piece of fast-burning charcoal. When I bow at the altar, I am not bowing down to gods or to powers that are outside of me. I am bowing to the enlightened qualities represented by each statue—qualities that also exist within me and within you.

Walking Meditation

Periods of sitting meditation can be interspersed with walking meditation. Walking meditation is similar to sitting, with the difference that we are now bringing an awareness of our breath together with our footsteps; we coordinate our steps with our breathing. With each in-breath we take a step with our right foot, and with each out-breath we take a step with our left. We walk slowly and deliberately, not forcing a relationship between steps and breath but allowing a harmonious relationship to develop.

If we are in a group, we walk in a line, one behind the other. You can let your hands hang down at your sides, or you can try adopting the more traditional hand position, as follows. Make a fist with your left hand, placing your thumb inside your fingers. Hold this fist with the palm facing in the direction of your solar plexus. Then place your right hand over and around your left fist, so that the left knuckles rest inside the right palm. In this position, place your right thumb on top of your left hand. Maintain this position as you walk, keeping your forearms parallel to the floor. You can also place your hands in gassho, that is, palms pressed together just in front of you with the tips of the second finger at a height even with the tip of your nose. Lower your gaze, letting it rest several feet in front of you.

Walk just to walk

There is no destination or goal. As you walk, bring yourself into the here and now with each step. Be aware of how your feet meet the floor. With each step we are touching the earth, connecting and communicating with it—and thereby with the whole universe. Notice any thoughts or feelings that arise, while also keeping an active awareness of your steps and your breath.

Especially in times of upset and worry, walking meditation is a wonderful tool to help us stay centered and focused and not get carried away by our thoughts, feelings, and perceptions. Just slow down and pay attention to your breath and your steps. Walking meditation is also a helpful support if you want to meditate for long periods of time. We can alternate periods of sitting meditation and walking meditation, which stretches and refreshes the body.

When doing walking meditation outside, follow the same guidelines, but walk a bit more quickly, connecting yourself to the pace of the larger world and of daily life. For example, breathe in for three steps and out for three steps, keeping in mind that the intention of walking meditation is always to allow for a natural rhythm of breath and steps to establish itself. (I have found that my own natural rhythm is four steps with each in-breath and four steps with each out-breath.)

While walking, allow yourself to experience the environment that you are moving through, that you are a part of. Notice how the air caresses or cools. Notice the colors that you move

through and your relationship to them, notice the sounds and your relationship to them. Be aware of your feet touching the ground as you walk, making contact with the earth with each step. Walk, breathe, and notice. When our mind wanders off, we bring our attention back to our steps and our breath. It can be helpful to incorporate walking meditation into your daily life, for example, doing it each day on the way to work or school can help settle the mind and can create a restorative transition.

Eating Meditation

We all have to eat, but often we don't pay much attention to what, how, and with whom we are eating. Eating in itself can become a drug that numbs our feelings and prevents us from waking up. The best preparation for eating meditation is to be hungry and to know that less is often more supportive to us than more.

When you sit down with a plate of food, before you begin eating, take a moment and breathe in and out consciously three times. Then recite the following verse out loud or internally, with your hands in gassho, concluding the verse with a half bow:

This food is a gift of the whole universe: the earth, the sky, and much hard work.

May we live in a way that makes us worthy to receive it.

May we transform our unskillful states of mind, especially our greed.

May we take only foods that nourish us and prevent illness.

We accept this food so that we may realize the path of practice of love, compassion, and peace.

Begin eating, making an effort to slow down the process. If possible, eat in silence. Chew each bite of food fifty times. Most of us swallow our food very quickly, barely chewing it at all. For many of us, it is the same dynamic in our lives: we don't want to chew on things. We rush through life's experiences, consuming things, pushing them in and down. So, take the time to appreciate the wonderful gift of food—the smells, tastes, looks, sounds. As you eat, stay in contact with your breath. Notice any thoughts and feelings that arise. Notice also how these thoughts and feelings then can give birth to perceptions, which we often experience as absolute truth and drive our action. Eating can be a quite vulnerable experience, which is perhaps why we so often rush through it or seek to distract ourselves from it. See what you can discover about the process of eating.

In eating meditation, make choices that help you to fully experience the food you eat. Rather than just eating for taste and pleasure, consider the health of your body and mind. Food is only healthy if there is a beneficial balance; too much doesn't work, too little doesn't work. In our Zen tradition, we make a commitment to not eat meat, fish, or poultry as a manifestation of our vow not to kill and not to support institutions of killing. We also look for ways to support animal welfare and the environment that sustains us.

Take fifteen minutes at each meal to practice eating meditation and your body will actually have a chance to inform you when it has had enough—a point we often miss. Your body

will be grateful to receive food that is properly chewed, and it will be grateful not to get too much or too little. If you are eating with children, you can promote appreciation and awareness of the food by beginning the meal with naming the foods on the table and acknowledging those who prepared it and the effort it took.

At the end of a period of eating meditation, breathe in and out three times and say out loud or internally, "Thank you." Or you can recite this closing verse, with your hands in gassho, ending it with a half bow:

May we exist in muddy water with purity like the lotus.
Thus we bow to Buddha.

Working Meditation

Whether at home or in the workplace, there is always work to be done, so we might as well use these tasks as opportunities to bring our meditation practice into our daily lives. Work, in one form or another, is ever-present in our lives, and it can become a wonderful expression of our creativity and of our connectedness with all life.

In working meditation, we stay connected with our breath as we work, and we work just to work, not to get a task done and off our list. We are not working to be done with something or to achieve something. We just do what is in front of us to do with our full awareness and staying in contact with our breath.

To begin working meditation, select a task and gather any tools needed to complete it. As you do a task, whether it is cleaning the dishes, cutting the grass, or conducting a business meeting, take the time to notice all the details—how things look, feel, smell. Be aware of what you perceive to be pleasant or unpleasant. Notice all the thoughts, feelings, and sensations that arise as you work. If you notice yourself getting lost in thought or rushing to complete the task, slow yourself down, reminding yourself to stay connected with your breath.

Recognize when and where you feel off balance and take a step toward more balance. For example, if you are someone who always works alone, ask someone for help. If you keep yourself mostly on the sidelines and let others take initiative, then be a little more assertive. If you have a tendency to work too quickly, slow down.

When you reach the end of a period of working meditation, take the time to care for the tools you used. For example, clean your tools and restore them to location where you found them. Taking care of the implements that support our work and our lives is a way of acknowledging them and expressing our gratitude toward them.

A Chinese Zen monk said: "A day without work is a day without food." Remember that our work supports us, makes our lives possible. Without an active engagement in daily life, such simple necessities as food will not magically appear. We can think of our work as a way to say thanks to the world for providing shelter, food, light, warmth, water, and so forth. Unfortunately, work has become a tremendous source of suffering in our society. Our worth, social acceptance, and belonging are often measured by what kind of job we have or whether we have a job at all. Working meditation can help us bring the light of awareness and compassion into the world of work.

Deep Listening and Mindful Speech

So much of our suffering gets acted out through the ways we communicate and relate to one another. The practice of deep listening and mindful speech helps us to become more aware during the process of speaking and listening. It supports us in receiving others' truths and in giving voice to our own. This practice is not always comfortable and easy, but it is essential to waking up and bringing an end to the repeating cycles of suffering we see in the world.

In this practice, we sit in a circle. An object—any object will do—is placed in the center of the group, and then we sit together for three cycles of breath (one cycle of breath is an in-breath followed by an out-breath). Next, when someone in the group is moved to speak, that person silently signals to the group that he or she is going to pick up the object. I often suggest that this person place the palms of the hands together in front of them in gassho and bow, but any gesture will do. It could be a wave of the hand. After completing the gesture, the speaker picks up the object, sits quietly for three cycles of breath, and then begins to talk, maintaining an awareness of the breath as an anchor.

The person holding the talking-object is empowered to speak, and the others in the group are empowered to listen. The listeners also use the breath as an anchor, paying attention to the thoughts that arise, the feelings, and the perceptions. Listeners do not comment or give advice, they simply breathe in and out, seeking to listen with their whole being—and to notice what prevents or disturbs their ability to listen. When finished speaking, the speaker gestures to the group in some way, perhaps in the same way as when picking up the object and places the object back in the center of the group. At this point the one who has been speaking becomes an active listener.

When speaking, use only I statements: "I feel...," "I notice...," and so forth. Avoid speaking in universal or general terms: beginning statements with "he/she," "they/them," or "you." When speaking, it's not a time for philosophizing, theorizing, or sharing political or religious beliefs. It's a time to speak authentically from a place of self, a place of shin, of heart-mind.

The group can select a topic for the practice period, or participants can speak about whatever seems important to them at that time. Examples of topics include:

- Why have I come to Zen practice?

- What prevents me from bringing meditation into my daily life?

- How do I experience loneliness (anger, fear)?

If the person who is speaking becomes emotional, the listeners are encouraged not interfere with this process, not to offer traditional gestures of comfort. No patting them on the back or handing them a tissue—unless the speaker specifically asks for that. Often these kinds of "comforting" gestures arise from the listener's discomfort and desire to stop the other from being emotional. In the practice of deep listening, we allow others to have their feelings and express them fully, without interruption, and we pay attention to the impulses and feelings that arise in us as we listen.

What is said in these groups must stay within the group in order to create a sense of safety and privacy. These are not discussion groups, and so at no point is there to be any cross talk, commenting, or advice giving. This is a disciplined practice to foster active listening.

Deep listening is about much more than taking in sound through our ears. Most of us have never had any instruction on how to truly listen to another person. Ordinarily, when we think we are listening to others, we are actually just thinking about how to respond. We might also be thinking of how we would like to change the other. In deep listening, we take a different approach. The essence of deep listening is:

1. To be aware of what I feel, what I am thinking, and how my thoughts and feelings give rise to perceptions as I listen.

2. To know that my feelings are my own and not necessarily those of the speaker.

3. To recognize that it is not my responsibility to fix, comfort, or heal the other person.

4. To understand that most communication is nonverbal.

With this approach, true listening becomes possible.

In our Zen lineage, we regularly recite the invocation of Avalokiteshvara, the bodhisattva who became enlightened by "hearing the sounds of the world." This invocation describes the approach and the value of deep listening.

We evoke your name, Avalokiteshvara. We aspire to learn your way, which is to listen in order to lessen the suffering in the world. You know how to listen in order to understand. We shall sit and listen without any prejudice. We shall sit and listen without judging and without reacting. We shall practice listening so attentively that we are able to hear what the other is saying and also what is left unsaid. We know that just by listening deeply we already alleviate a great deal of the pain and suffering in the other.

Learning to listen in this way is an essential aspect of bringing meditation to life: bringing it off the cushion and into everything that we do, all of the time.

As with all forms of practice, this is an ongoing, open-ended process. We can begin by noticing what gets in the way of listening deeply. Am I missing what's being said because I'm planning what I want to say? Am I thinking about how to fix or rescue the other person? If I notice that I'm doing any of that, I can stop, consciously bring my attention back to my breath, and just listen.

Let's listen to each other, really listen, without trying to change or fix anything. As we listen, let's just offer our openness and companionship. This is the beginning of the journey toward healing. Though we may think that we know how to listen, often when other people talk, we don't manage to really listen. We tend to judge what's being said, defend ourselves, react, offer advice, or seek to control the situation in some way. So, a disciplined practice of listening will be helpful.

In emphasizing the value of speaking and listening, I want to point out the importance of realizing that healing doesn't happen to someone who has suffered trauma, it happens by someone who has suffered trauma. In our society we are led to believe that something outside of ourselves heals us—a physician, a therapist, a preacher, God. In reality, we are responsible for our own healing. We need tools to help us on our path, and they are rooted in spiritual practice, rooted in the truth that we cannot hide from our suffering or eradicate it, but we can learn to be at peace with our unpeacefulness.

Sleeping Meditation

When we lay in our bed, or wherever we choose to or have the opportunity to engage in this practice, it is important to be aware of the necessity and gift of rest. As you lay down to sleep, place your arms and hands at your side or rest them on your belly breathing in and breathing out with awareness. Allow your body to relax into the experience of sleep. Sleeping just to sleep.

    I suffered for years because of my rigid expectations surrounding how I was supposed to sleep: that a normal or healthy night's sleep consisted of a minimum of 8 hours of uninterrupted sleep. This is not my reality. Before I was introduced to Zen practice, I grasped for external solutions to make my sleep pattern conform to this standard, and I suffered. As a result of my disciplined, committed, and sustained application of the practices that are described in this book, I came to an awareness that the way I sleep is my standard, and that I was getting good enough rest.

    There are times when I am visited in dreams by situations that are very unsettling, sometimes so unsettling that I am not able to relax back into sleep. In these moments I have been able to develop strategies, rooted in practice, that support me. Sometimes I sit in meditation, sometimes I do walking meditation, sometimes I clean (working meditation), sometimes I read. I experiment, allowing myself to be informed by the experience of these moments until I am able to settle and lay back down. There are times within these experiences that I am simply not able to lay back down. In these moments I carry the knowledge that I will at some point be able to rest.

Also, while practicing sleeping meditation, it is important to be aware of your impact on others. We practice sleeping meditation in strict silence. If that is not possible, then please place yourself where you don't disturb others. This is also the practice of meditation: to be aware that I do not stop at my skin, that my actions touch all that is around me, that my actions affect the whole universe.

Leave No Trace

An important aspect of an active meditation practice is caring for the spaces we inhabit. Take the time throughout the day to clean up after yourself, paying attention to the details. Before you leave a space that you've used, tidy up and restore it in such a way that the next person would not know that you had been there.

This practice begins when we first wake up in the morning. Make the bed as if you had never slept in it. I do this every time I get out of a bed, no matter what. With this practice I am expressing how thankful I am to have a bed to sleep in because for me this hasn't always been the case.

When using the bathroom also leave no traces. At the bathroom sink, keep a small towel for wiping down and drying the sink and the faucet after each use. After taking a shower, use a squeegee on the shower walls and then a small towel to dry the walls, fixtures, and the bottom of the shower. Don't leave any water droplets or stray hairs. As you clean up after yourself, take the time to appreciate how the bathroom supports you, day in and day out. Show your appreciation by caring for it. In this way we also show care and respect for the next person who uses the bathroom after us.

In the kitchen, after preparing a meal or a snack, don't leave dirty dishes in the sink. Take the time to wash all the dishes, utensils, pots and pans with careful attention, putting everything back in its place. As you clean up, notice how all the items you have used have helped you to nourish yourself. Finish by wiping down the countertops and cleaning and drying the sink.

The practice of leaving no traces runs against our typical fast-paced, buy-it-and-throw-it-away culture. It slows us down and encourages us not to just use up the items we own and the spaces we inhabit. We move from being the consumers of our possessions to being their caretakers.

In these tumultuous times, people often ask me what they can do to create positive change in the world. I often suggest that they begin by making their bed in the morning as if they never slept in it. This might sound trivial, but the practice of leaving no traces is profound and transformative. How we go about caring for the spaces we live in is directly connected to how we care for ourselves and for our world.

I find inspiration in the recorded teachings of the 10th century Chinese Zen monk Fayan Wenyi. One of the lessons I have drawn from his teaching is: *If a thing is not practical, it is not spiritual.* Zen is not about what we think, say, or believe. It is about what we do. We cannot think our way into a new way of living. We must live our way into a new way of thinking.

Be on Time

Whenever we gather for formal Zen practice, I emphasize the importance of being on time, which in our community means being seated and settled on the cushion or chair five minutes before the practice period is scheduled to begin. When people are late, we ask them to wait outside the zendo until we transition to the next form of practice.

Over the years, I have found that showing up five minutes early—not just for practice periods but for any appointment—helps the day's schedule to proceed more smoothly and calmly. And yet the level of resistance that I encounter to this simple practice is remarkable. People often rush into the zendo seconds before we close the door, breathless and stressed. This rushing carries a chaotic energy that impacts the whole group. Being late also draws attention to oneself and, consciously or unconsciously, can be a way of seeking to control the group.

Being on time shows care and respect for the person or people I'm meeting, and it's another way to develop attention. Being on time requires me to cultivate an awareness of where I am in space and time. I need to pace my activities in such a way that I give myself enough time to get to my next commitment without rushing and creating unnecessary stress.

Some people are consistently late for practice and then get upset when they are asked to wait outside the zendo until the next period of practice. Often those who are late will argue or seek to justify their lateness. From time to time, despite our best intentions, we will be late. In such a case, we can simply take responsibility for being late without argument. When we are aware that we are running late, we can also show respect by notifying the other as soon as possible. This is courteous, puts the other at ease, and demonstrates that the appointment and person are important to us.

Make it your practice to arrive five minutes early for every appointment on your schedule, keeping in mind that meditation and daily life are not two things. See how this practice can invite more calmness into your life. Also, notice what distracts you from being on time. Are you unrealistic in your planning? Did you allow your phone to distract you? Notice if there's a pattern to what makes you late, and when you are late, be accountable and take responsibility.

Doorway Practice

At the first Buddhist monastery where I studied, the abbot taught me the practice of consciously and carefully opening and closing each doorway that I passed through. I still do this practice today. It slows me down, grounding me in the present and helping me to resist the urge to rush forward into whatever I imagine is next.

When approaching a doorway, pay attention to each detail of moving through it. Be aware of your body, of your hand reaching for the doorknob, taking hold of it, turning it, and opening the door. Watch your mind. Notice the thoughts and feelings that arise. Notice how they press you to blast forward in unawareness. Learn to be present with those feelings. Step through the doorway consciously. Notice how your whole world shifts and changes. It's as if you are moving from one universe to another. Be willing to experience it that way.

Then pay attention as you close the door. Notice the movements of your body as you reach for the doorknob on the opposite side of the door. Close the door with gentleness and care, then pay attention as you let go of the knob. Finish this process completely before turning to face the new space.

In the beginning this was an intense and difficult practice for me. The feelings that would rise up in me seemed explosive and unbearable. It sometimes felt like there was a swarm of buzzing bees inside my body, and I just wanted it to stop. I tried to avoid these kinds of feelings through constant activity and by focusing my attention on things outside of myself, things I had absolutely no control over. This practice helped me to slow down and learn the value of being present—and it helped me to understand what distracted me from being present.

It's interesting to watch visitors to the Magnolia Zen Center pass through the doorway of the zendo before they learn this practice. Most people move through the doorway absentmindedly. It's not unusual to see people burst through the doorway roughly and loudly, rushing to get to their cushions, neglecting to close the door behind them. They don't yet understand that meditation doesn't start or end on the cushion or chair.

Bring your full attention to these transitions from one space to another. Doorways provide us with frequent and wonderful opportunities to begin to live differently.

Goodbye Meditation

Whenever groups gather at the Magnolia Zen Center, whether in person or online, at the conclusion of any of the events, a point of emphasis is the saying of goodbye. Having been a soldier in war, I am deeply aware of the uncertainty and fragility of life. I take the time to say goodbye with my full attention because, in truth, I don't know if I'll ever see the other person again, and I don't want to miss the opportunity.

Saying goodbye is an intimate process. It touches feelings of loss and of grief. There was a time in my life when I avoided saying goodbye. I didn't know how to be present with the vulnerability of those moments, with the feelings that would rise up in me as I acknowledged this loss. I wasn't even aware that I had these feelings.

Over time, goodbyes have developed into a spiritual practice, another form of an active meditation practice. I usually begin a goodbye by bowing to the other, in *gassho*, and then expressing in words my care and appreciation for our time together. As with all forms of meditation, I stay in contact with my breath, noticing what arises in me and also what might distract me from staying present through the process. Saying goodbye is not unlike moving through a doorway. I pay attention as I proceed through this transition. I don't rush through it in an attempt to avoid discomfort. I slow down for goodbyes.

Saying goodbye offers me the opportunity to express my care and respect for the other while I still can. When done with my full attention and awareness, goodbyes express my wish to not take people, places, animals, or any connections for granted. It also reflects my willingness to recognize the reality of impermanence.

Paying attention to ordinary, daily goodbyes will support us when we have to face life's bigger changes and endings. In our Zen tradition, each evening we recite the following verse:

> Let me respectfully remind you:
> Life and death are of supreme importance.
> Time passes swiftly by and opportunity is lost.
> Each of us must strive to awaken.
> Awaken! Take heed! Do not squander this life!

Don't miss the everyday opportunities to say goodbye. Without a real goodbye, there cannot be a true hello.

Conclusion

In my experience people come to spiritual practice for all kinds of reasons, but at the center of these varied reasons rests a nagging sense of incompleteness, a sense that something is missing. People come to Zen practice looking to find some sort of meaning to their existence. This can happen (discovering meaning), but only genuinely within the context of the spiritual reality of life, which is cultivated and sustained through the discipline of spiritual practice.

Spiritual Practice requires an unwavering commitment and discipline because without this, nothing will change. Spiritual practice in and of itself is quite simple. It is rooted in the reality that if we want things to be different, we must live our lives differently somehow.

In my own practice, study, and teaching over the years, four essential aspects of Zen Buddhist practice have come to stand out to me.

1. Silence

The foundation of Zen practice is a committed, consistent, silent sitting meditation practice supported by an authentic teacher

and a practice community. Zen practice is about bringing more silence into our lives and about bringing the silence that is sitting meditation into everything we do. "Silence" in this sense doesn't just mean the absence of noise. Anyone who has sat in meditation understands that the workings of the mind, even in the absence of external sounds, can be deafening. The practice of silence is about noticing and changing our relationship with the internal and external noises that accompany us day and night, neither rejecting them nor attaching to them.

2. Discipline

An essential ingredient in our practice is the commitment and determination to keep going no matter what, to continue to sit just to sit, to walk to just walk, to eat just to eat, whether we feel like it or not. Along the way, we will encounter doubts and challenges. Our minds will tell us we don't really need to sit today, that it doesn't matter, or that it's not "working." Our discipline is to continue to practice each day—on and off the cushion—and see what unfolds.

3. Ritual

Part of a committed Zen practice is learning the rituals and services that have been handed down from teacher to student for generations. "The object of ceremony," according to the Sutra of Hui-neng, "is to curb arrogance." Our lives are full of ritual, not only in the meditation hall but throughout the day. Our practice is to approach everything we do in the zendo with great care and attention and then to carry that into all aspects of our daily lives.

4. Study

Our practice is deepened by reading classical Buddhist texts such as the Dhammapada, the Heart Sutra, the Diamond Sutra, the Lankavatara Sutra, the Platform Sutra, and the Avatamsaka Sutra. But we must remember that waking up is not an intellectual process. When studying these texts, we read just to read, keeping ever conscious that the heart of practice does not rest in the words but rather in the space between the words, in the space between the letters.

What is offered in this book are tools that will support us in the process of waking up, of living differently. But we have to use these tools consistently and without expectation of an imagined result. We must engage in these practice forms just to engage them; practicing just to practice. Through this effort we will eventually be provided with insight—insight into the nature of our suffering and the nature of our resistance to engaging the tools freely given through this teaching.

No one can do this for us. We are responsible, one by one, to bring meditation to life in everything we do, to see what prevents us from doing this, and to then do something different. We have the choice and the opportunity to live differently, to become more directly and fully present in our lives.

About the Author

Claude AnShin Thomas is a decorated Vietnam combat veteran turned Zen Buddhist monk, author, and speaker. Trained in a Vietnamese Zen monastery and in the White Plum lineage of Japanese Soto Zen, Claude AnShin communicates Zen Buddhist teachings in a non-religious manner that is direct and drawn from life, with a deep-rooted sense of compassion and purpose. He is the author of the award-winning book *At Hell's Gate: A Soldier's Journey from War to Peace* and more recently of *Bringing Meditation to Life: 108 Teachings on the Path of Zen Practice* and *On the Edges of Sleep: Poems of War and Memory*.

International Work

Claude AnShin Thomas divides his time between the U.S., Europe, and South America, speaking about the real costs of war and violence and how meditation practice can support healing and transformation. He is dedicated to bringing awareness to the culture of violence in and among individuals, families, societies, and countries.

His intimate and deep understanding of the nature of suffering has allowed him to serve people in a wide variety of settings including war zones, hospitals, schools, and prisons. He has led meditation retreats at sites of war and suffering, and he communicates with paramilitaries, gang members, guerrillas, and refugees. He offers public talks and retreats that help participants to recognize and end repetitive cycles of suffering.

Work with Veterans

Claude AnShin Thomas regularly leads meditation retreats for veterans living with post traumatic stress and moral injury. At these retreats, offered in locations around the U.S., veterans and their family members learn to practice meditation in a variety of forms including sitting, walking, working, eating, and writing, allowing them to begin the process of rebuilding their lives.

Academic Work

Claude AnShin Thomas has been a guest teacher and scholar-in-residence at Moravian College in Bethlehem, Pennsylvania, and Allegheny College in Meadville, Pennsylvania. Claude AnShin Thomas holds a BS in English Education from Slippery Rock University (Slippery Rock, PA), an MSM from Lesley University (Cambridge, MA), and an honorary Doctorate in Divinity from Moravian College (Bethlehem, PA).

Stay Connected

Join Our E-Mail List

Find out about retreats and other events and get the latest news about the work of Claude AnShin Thomas and the Zaltho Foundation. Visit www.zaltho.org to sign up.

Subscribe to Our Podcast

The Zaltho Live podcast ZalthoLIVE presents dharma talks and dialogues with Zen monk Claude AnShin Thomas exploring how Buddhist teachings and meditation practice can be brought to bear in all aspects of our lives. Now available on Apple iTunes, Spotify, Google Podcast, Amazon Music/Audible, and at www.zaltho.org.

Follow Us on Facebook and Instagram

Look for the Zaltho Foundation on Facebook and Instagram to access new audio and video teachings from Claude AnShin Thomas as they become available; enjoy short, inspirational teachings; and stay up-to-date on community news and events.

Also Available

At Hell's Gate: A Soldier's Journey From War to Peace

In this raw and moving memoir, Claude AnShin Thomas describes his service in Vietnam, his subsequent emotional collapse, and his remarkable journey toward healing. "Everyone has their Vietnam," Thomas writes. "Everyone has their own experience of violence, calamity, or trauma." This book offers timeless teachings on how we can all find healing, with practical guidance on how mindful awareness and compassion can transform our lives.

"Claude Anshin Thomas has been an inspiration to me. Our world urgently needs to listen to him tell of his life in war and then in peace."

—Maxine Hong Kingston, author of *The Woman Warrior*

"Written with relentless courage and utter compassion, this account of violence and transformation is one of the most amazing and wonderful stories I've ever read."

—Michael Herr, Vietnam War correspondent and author of *Dispatches*

Bringing Meditation to Life: 108 Teachings on the Path of Zen Practice

Presented in 108 short, to-the-point, provocative chapters, this book offers essential instruction on sitting meditation practice and how it can inform our relationships, communication, conflicts, peace work, and more. Interspersed throughout the book are some of the author's favorite quotes from Zen literature.

"Claude AnShin distills the wisdom he has earned through the practice of meditation and a remarkable life devoted to the dharma, peacemaking, and serving others. This is a book, and a rare teacher, worthy of our trust."
—**Charles Johnson, winner of the National Book Award and author of** *Turning the Wheel: Essays on Buddhism and Writing*

"Shorn of mystification and cultural accretions, this is an elegant book which I recommend to students new to Zen and to those who wish to go deeper."
—**Hozan Alan Senauke, abbot of Berkeley Zen Center, author of** *The Bodhisattva's Embrace: Dispatches from Engaged Buddhism's Front Lines*

"This book is a must read for anyone walking the path of peace and justice."
—**Genjo Marinello, abbot of Chobo-ji Zen Temple, Seattle**

On the Edges of Sleep: Poems of War and Memory

In his first book of poetry, combat veteran and Zen monk Claude AnShin Thomas explores the boundaries of awareness; the landscape of longing; and the lasting, invisible wounds of war.

"A revelatory and therapeutic experience for spiritual seekers, victims of trauma, and a must-read for those impacted by war."

—**Camillo Mac Bica, author of *Beyond PTSD: The Moral Casualties of War***

www.ingramcontent.com/pod-product-compliance
Lightning Source LLC
Chambersburg PA
CBHW020545080526
44583CB00013B/1005